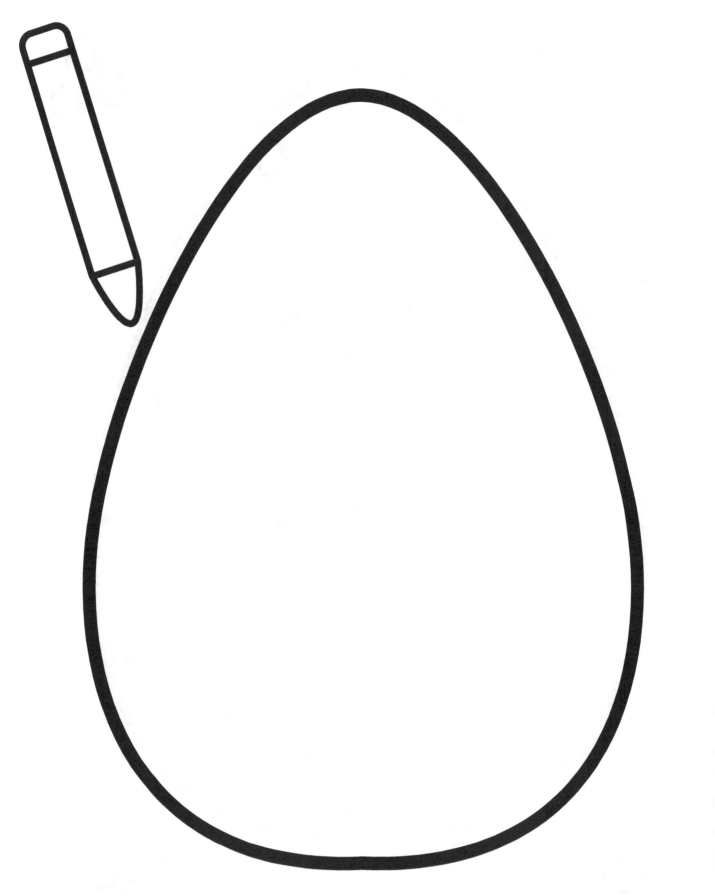

DRAW AND COLOR

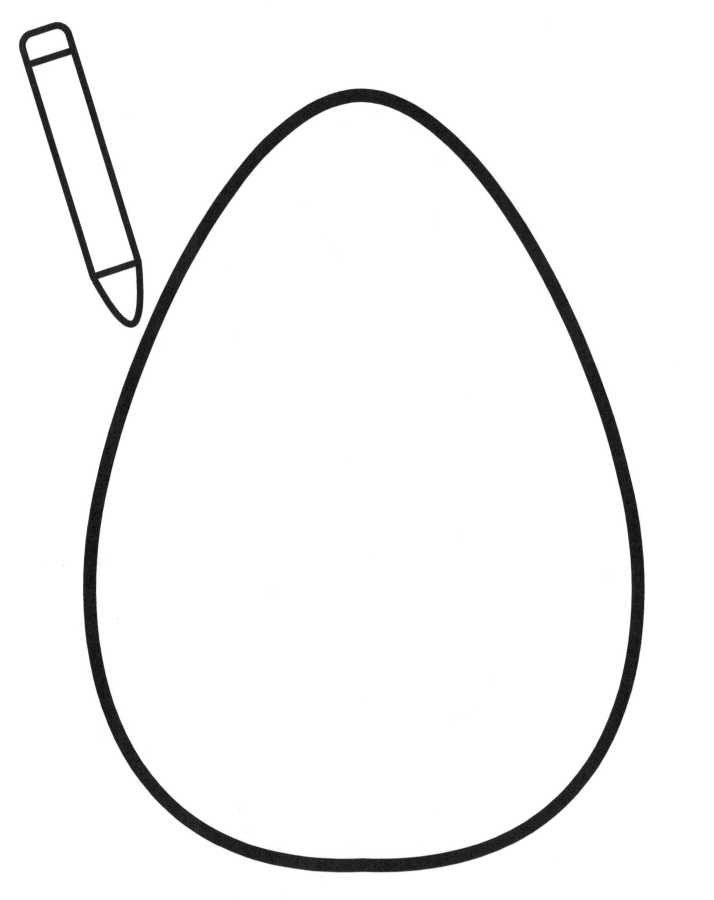

DRAW AND COLOR

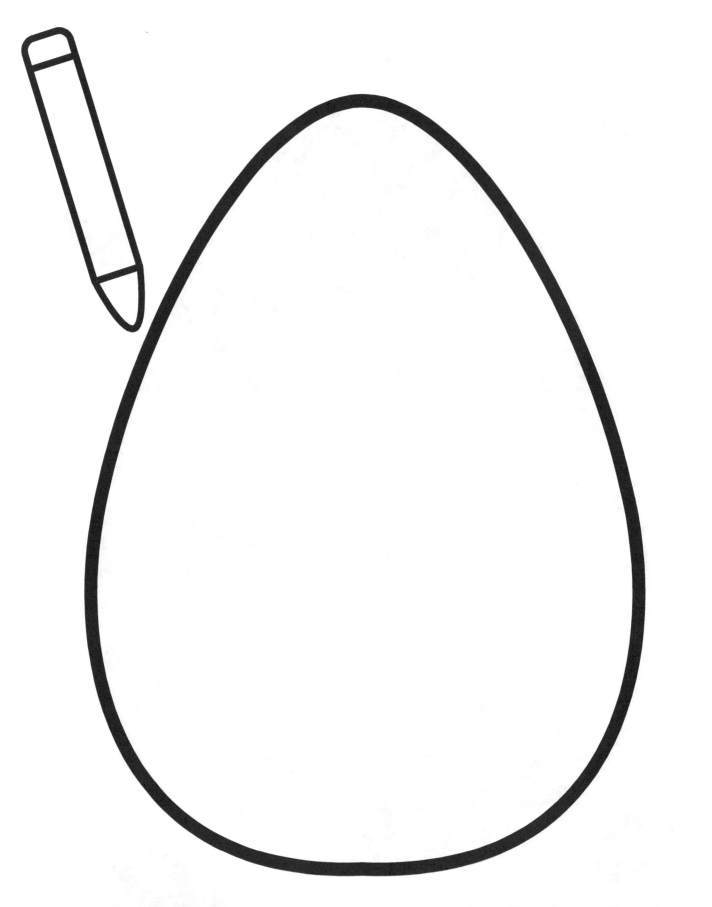

DRAW AND COLOR

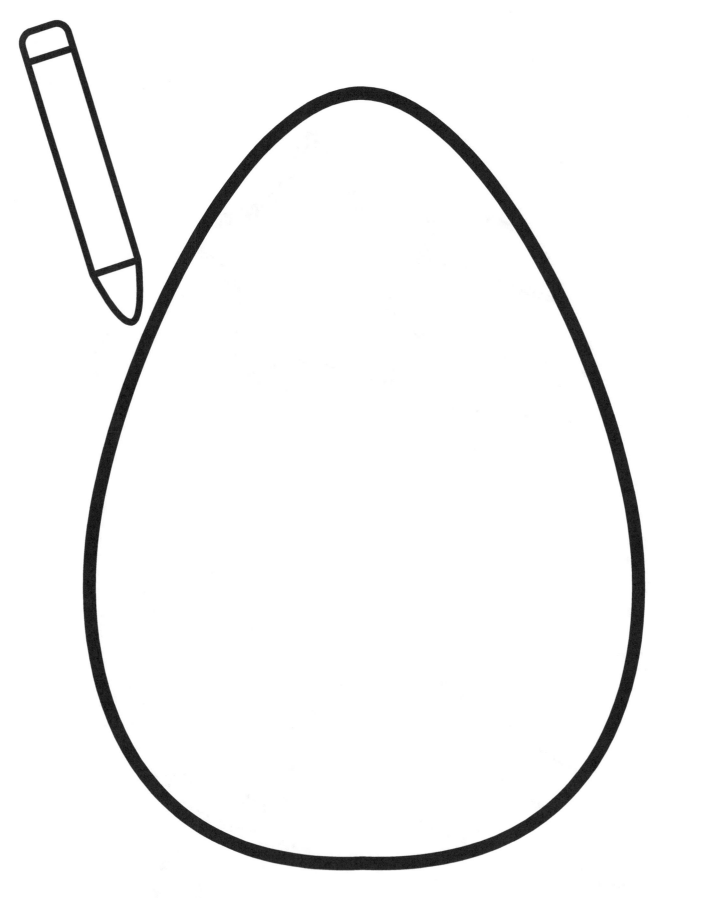

DRAW AND COLOR

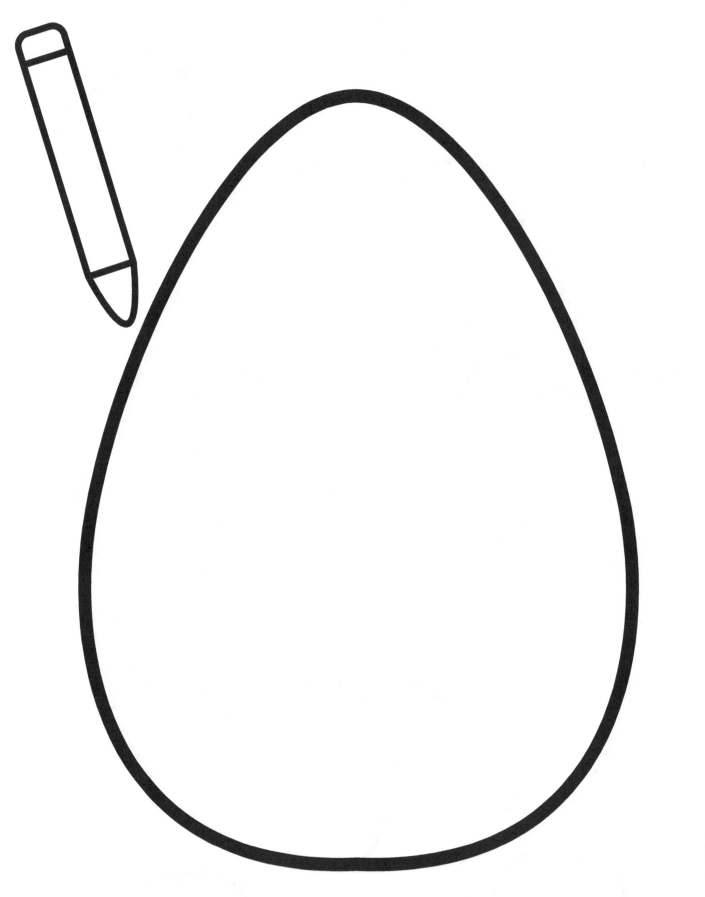

DRAW AND COLOR

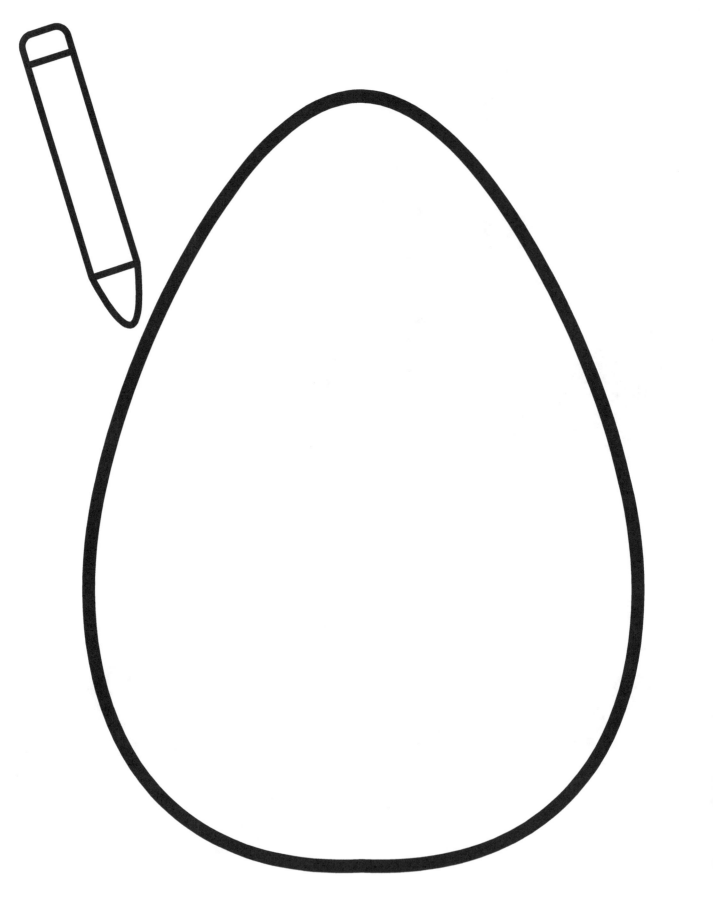

DRAW AND COLOR

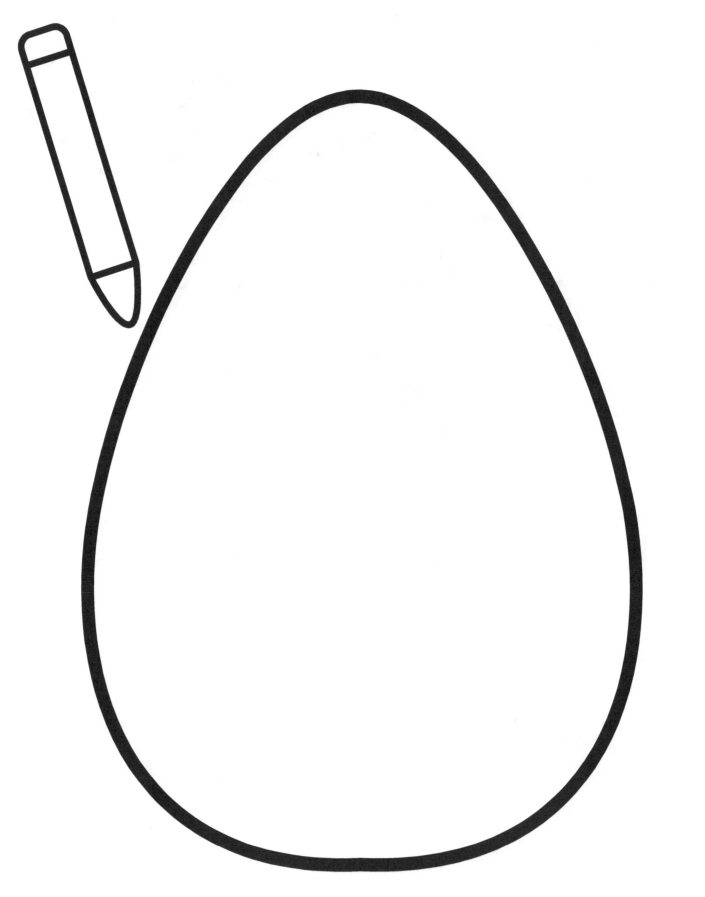

DRAW AND COLOR

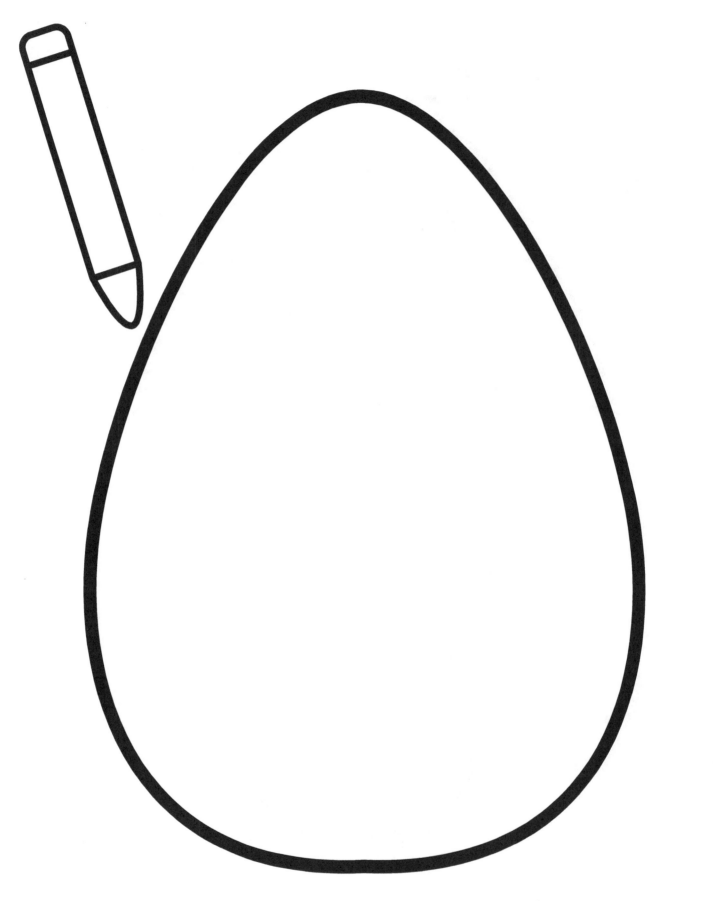

DRAW AND COLOR

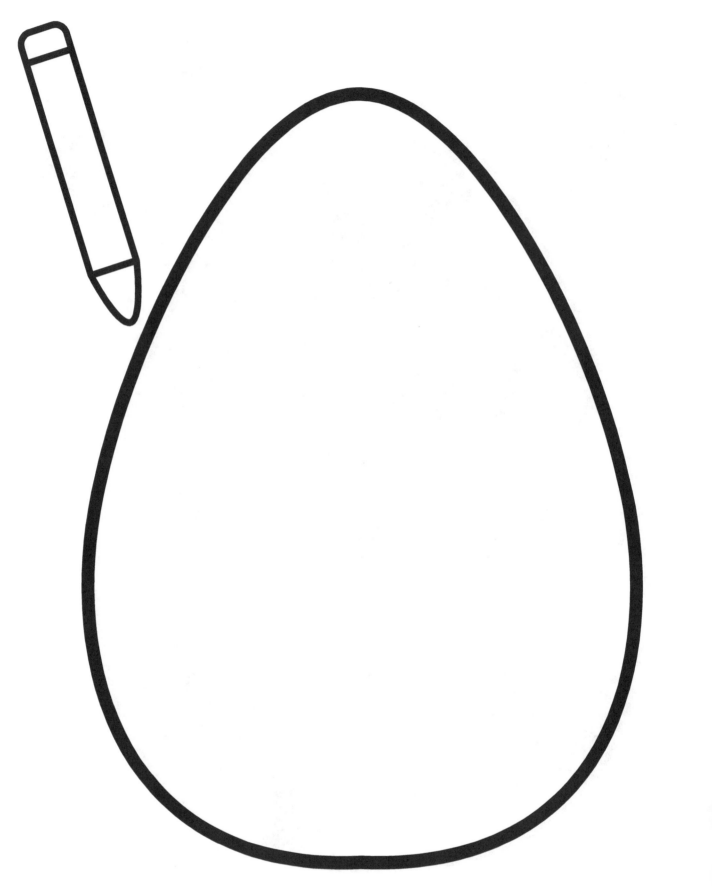

DRAW AND COLOR

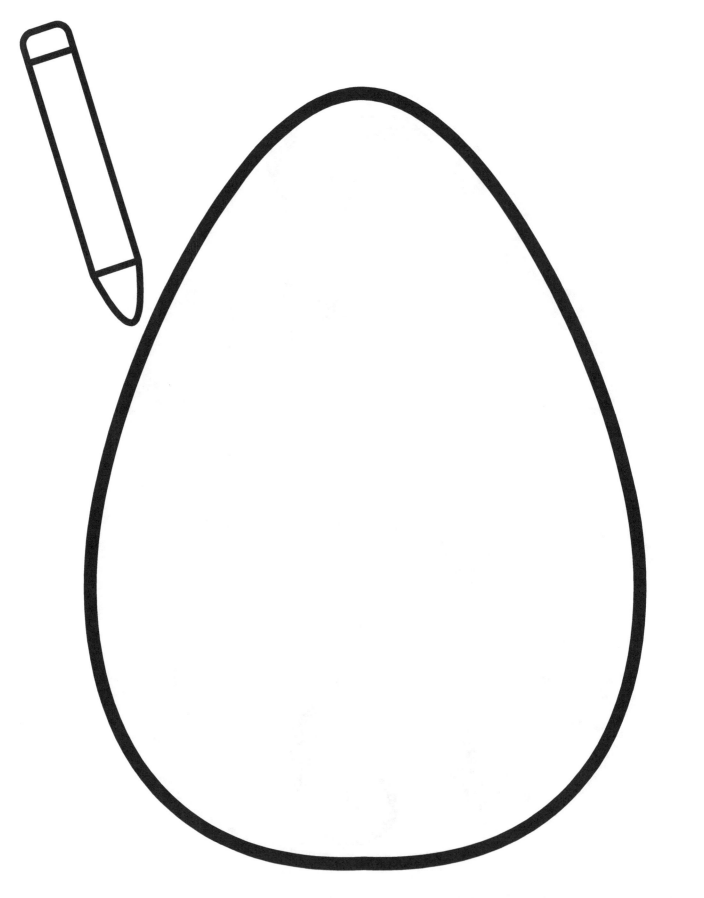

DRAW AND COLOR

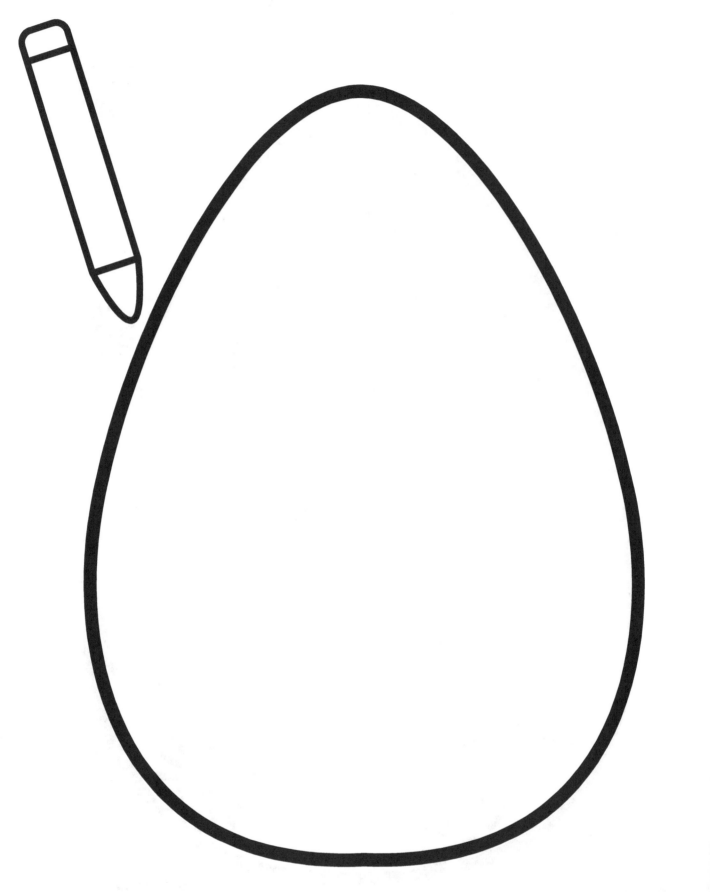

DRAW AND COLOR

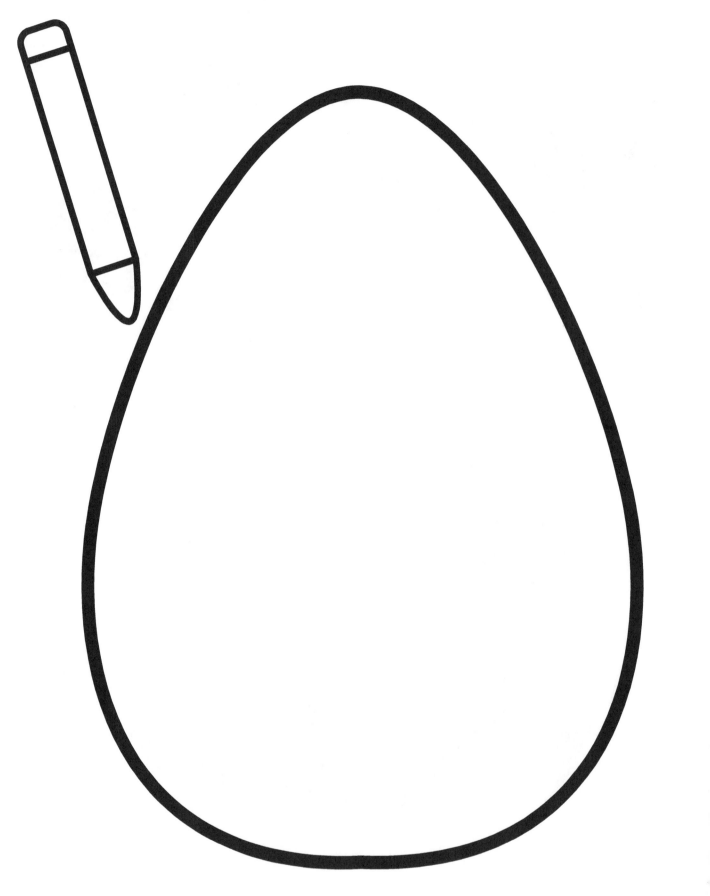

DRAW AND COLOR

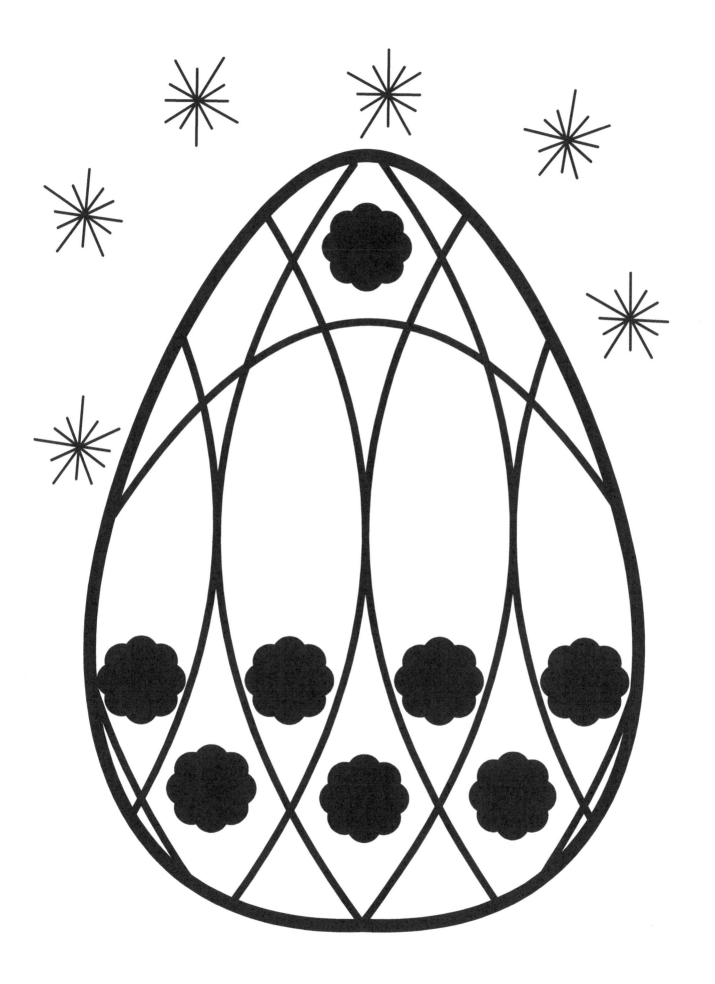

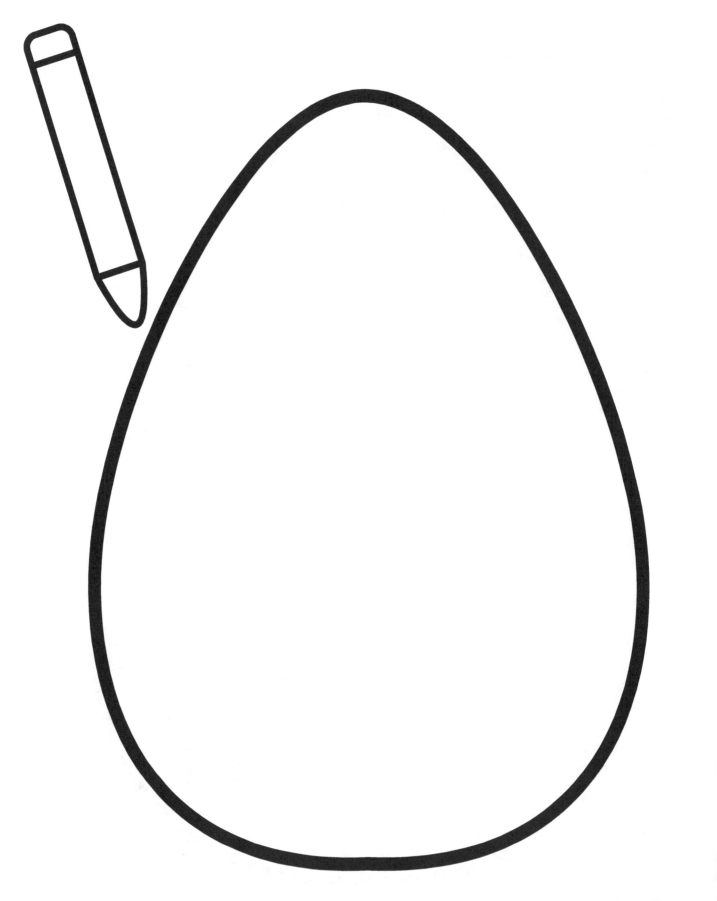

DRAW AND COLOR

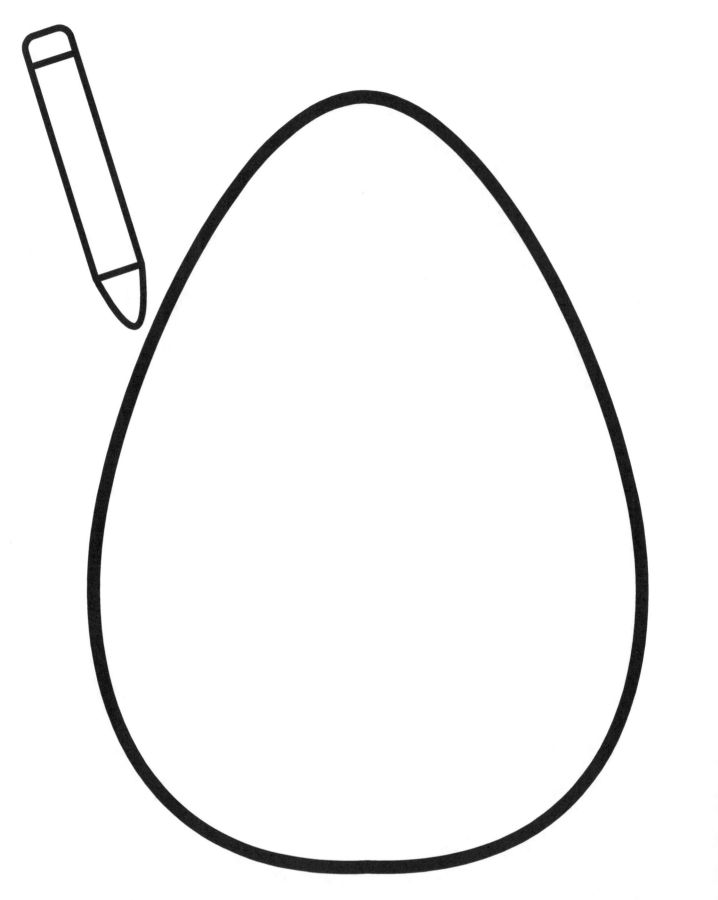

DRAW AND COLOR

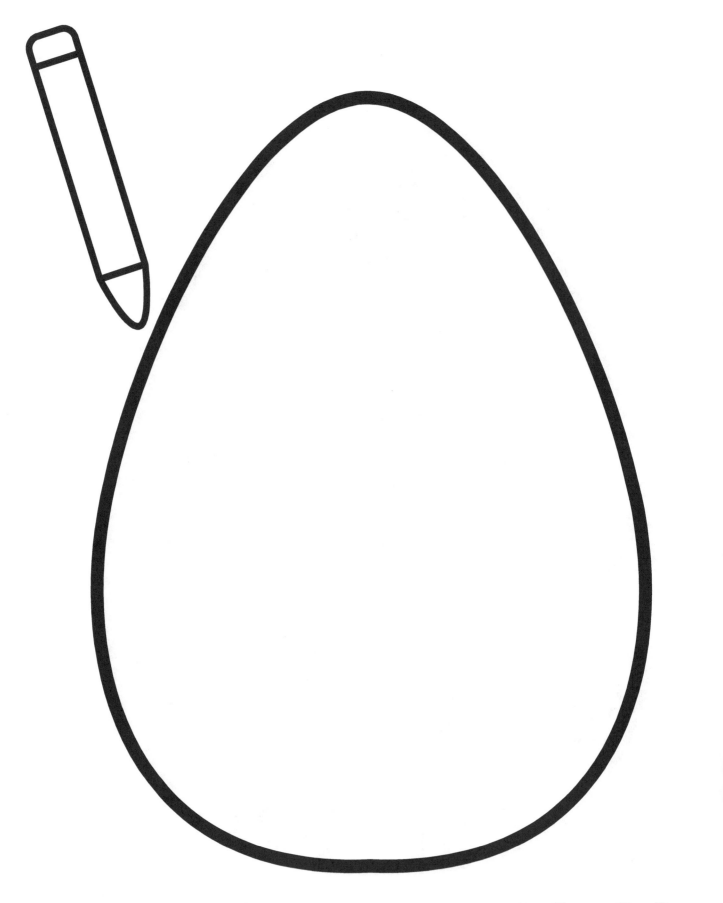

DRAW AND COLOR

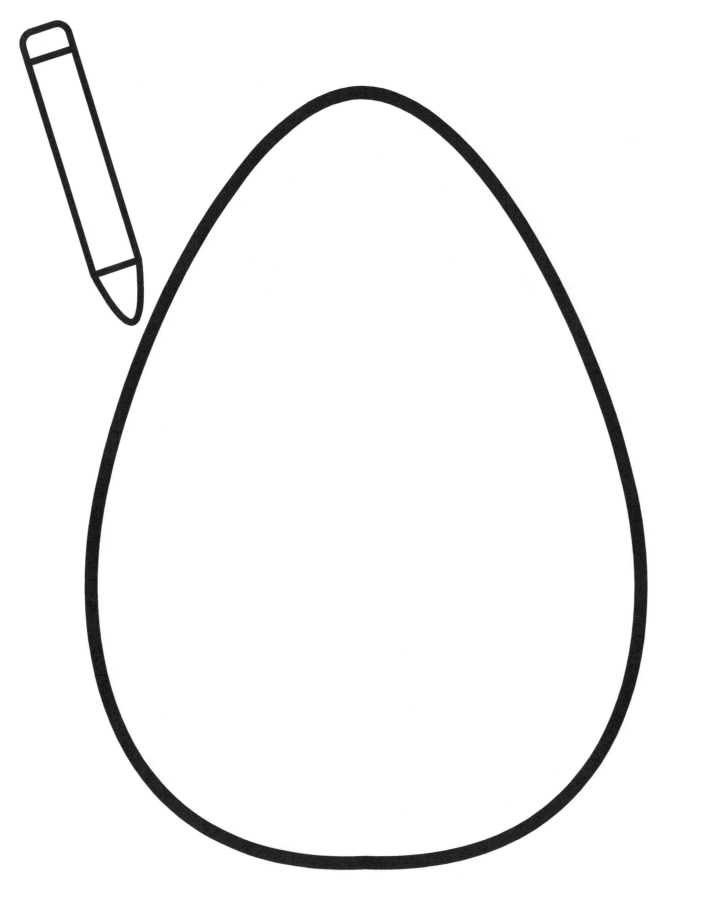

DRAW AND COLOR

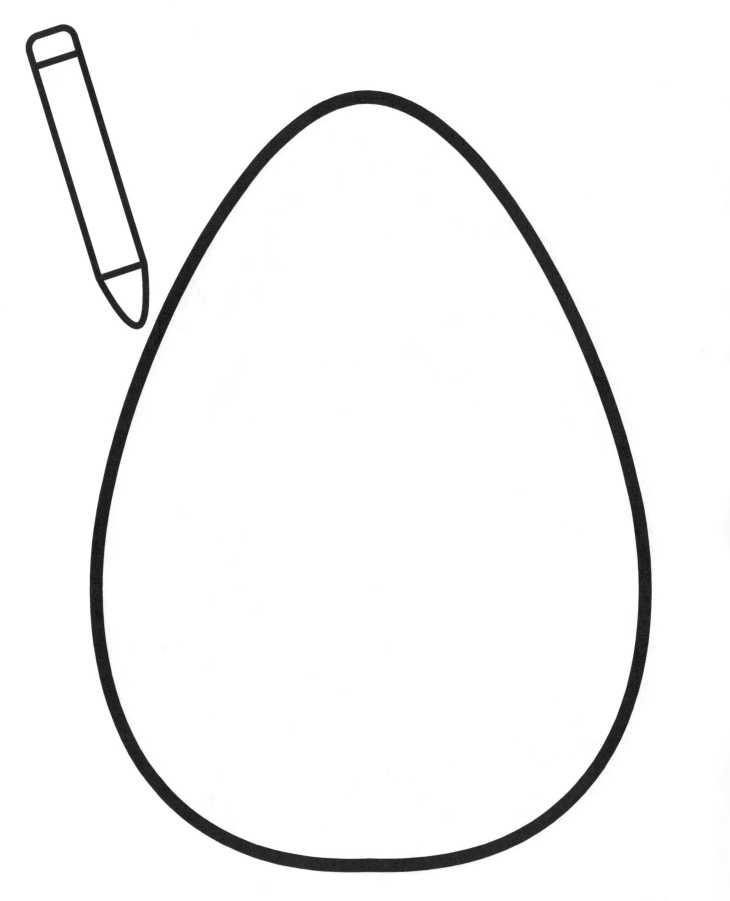

DRAW AND COLOR

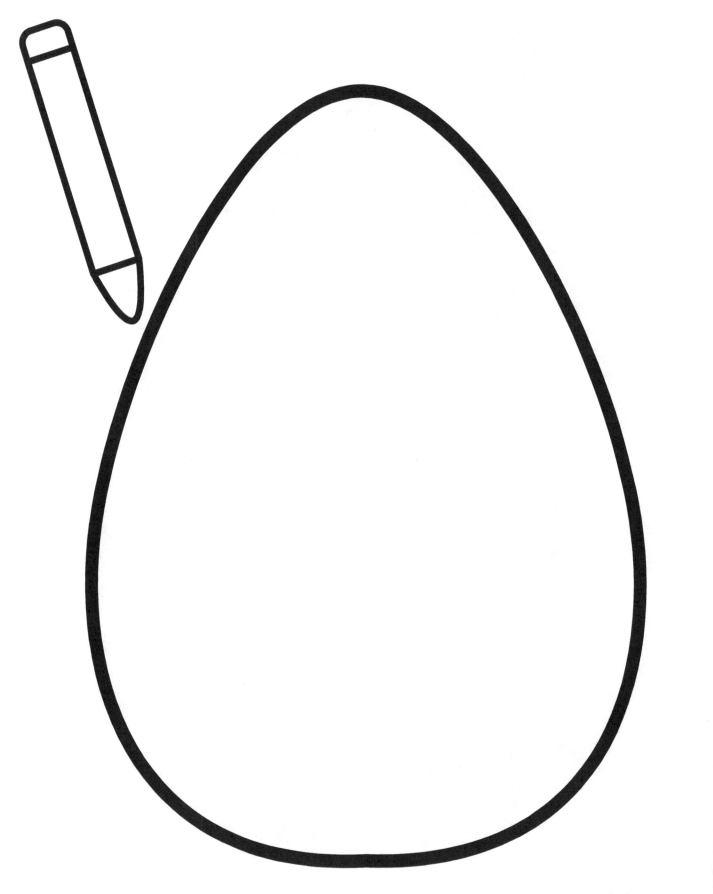

DRAW AND COLOR

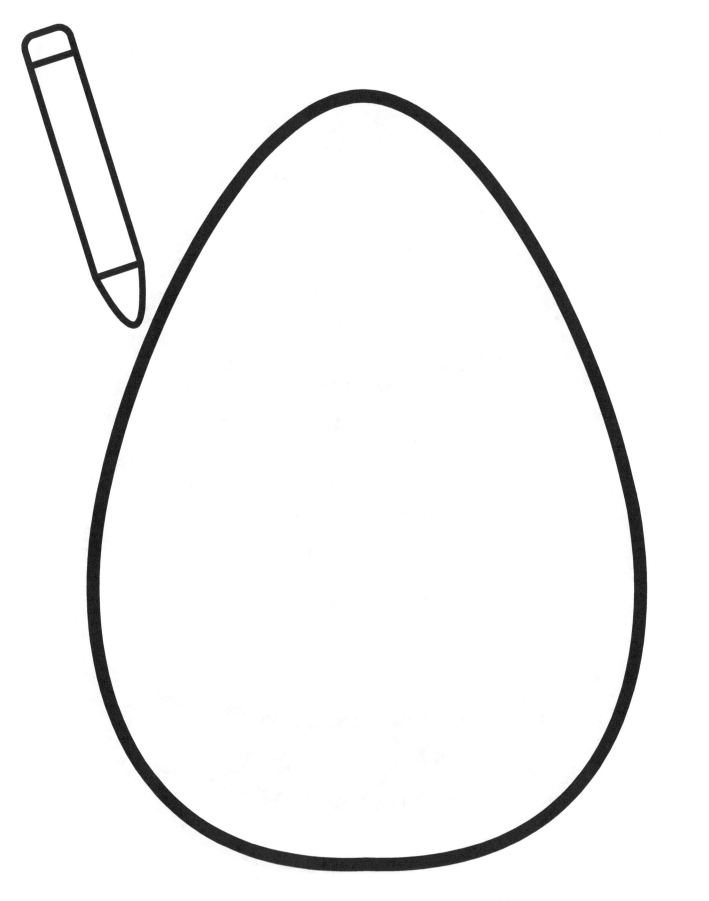

DRAW AND COLOR

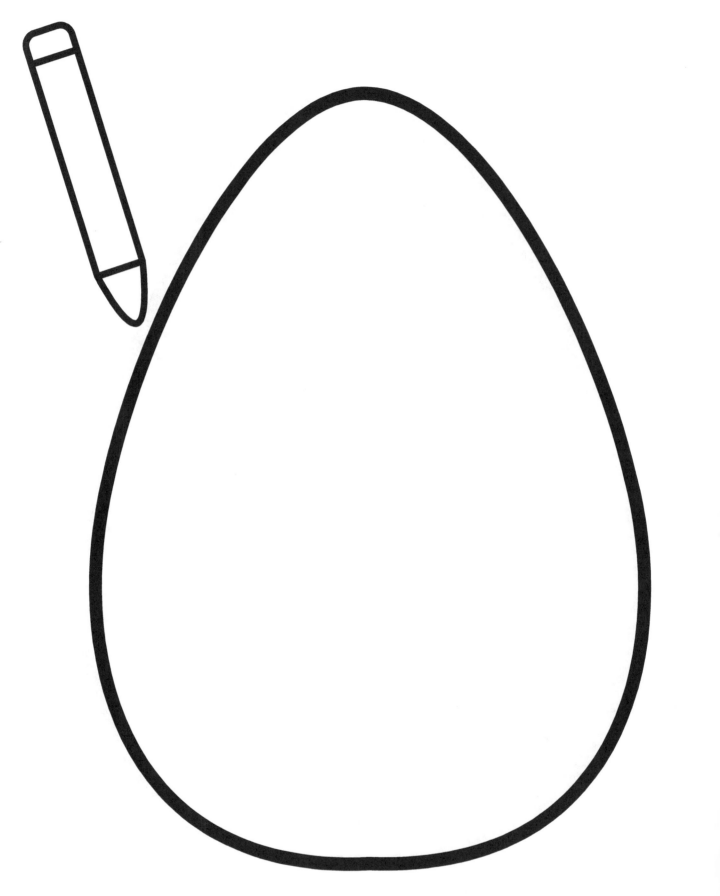

DRAW AND COLOR

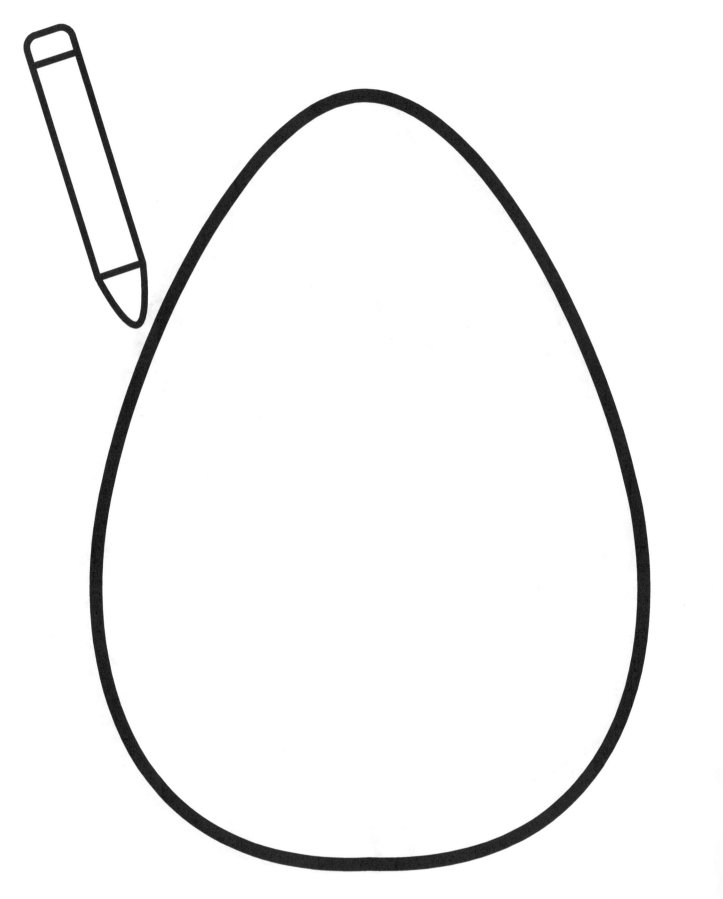

DRAW AND COLOR

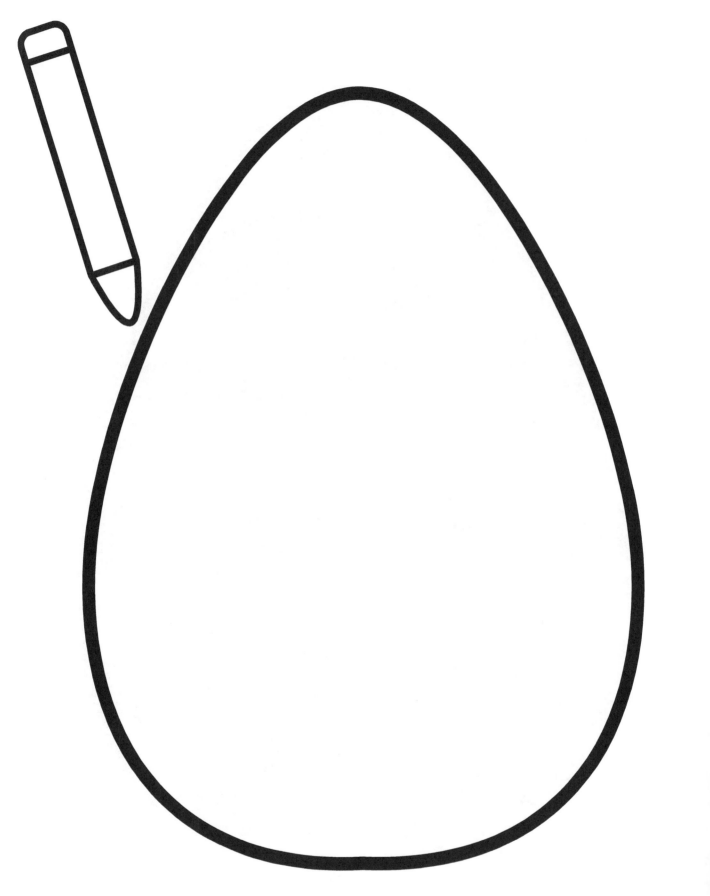

DRAW AND COLOR

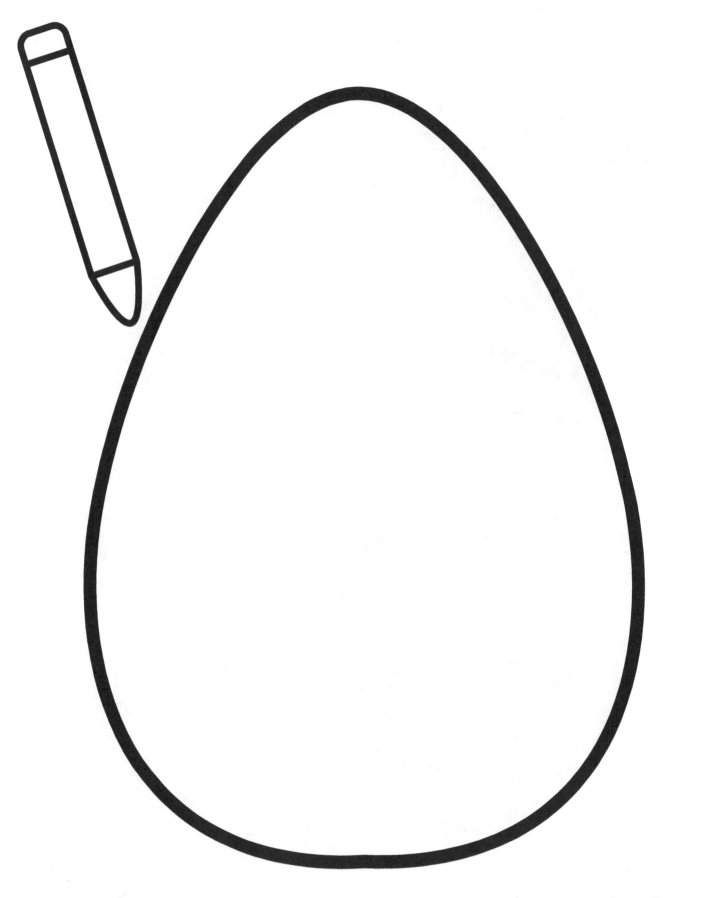

DRAW AND COLOR

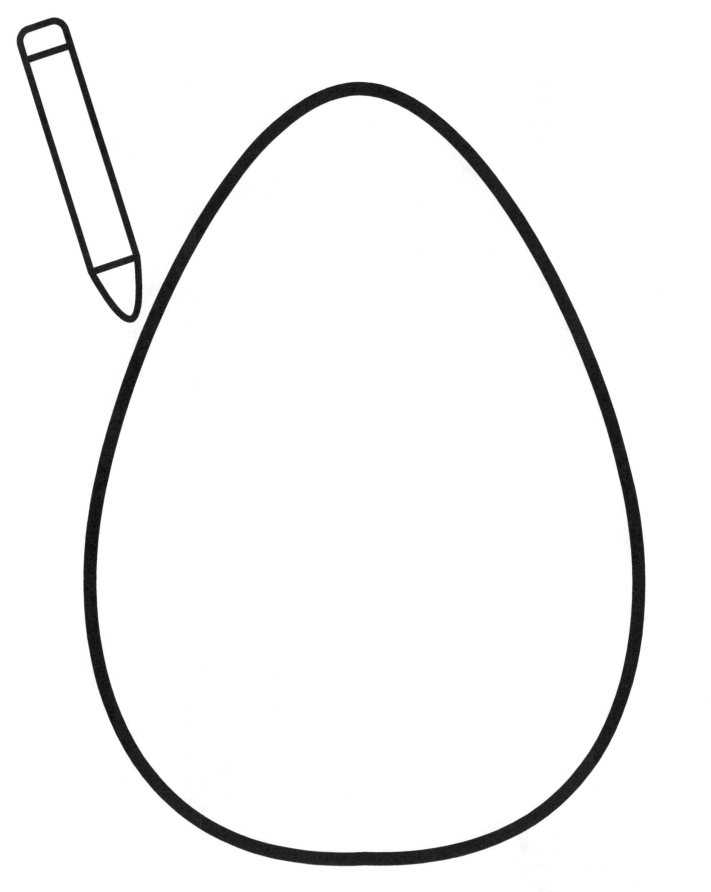

DRAW AND COLOR

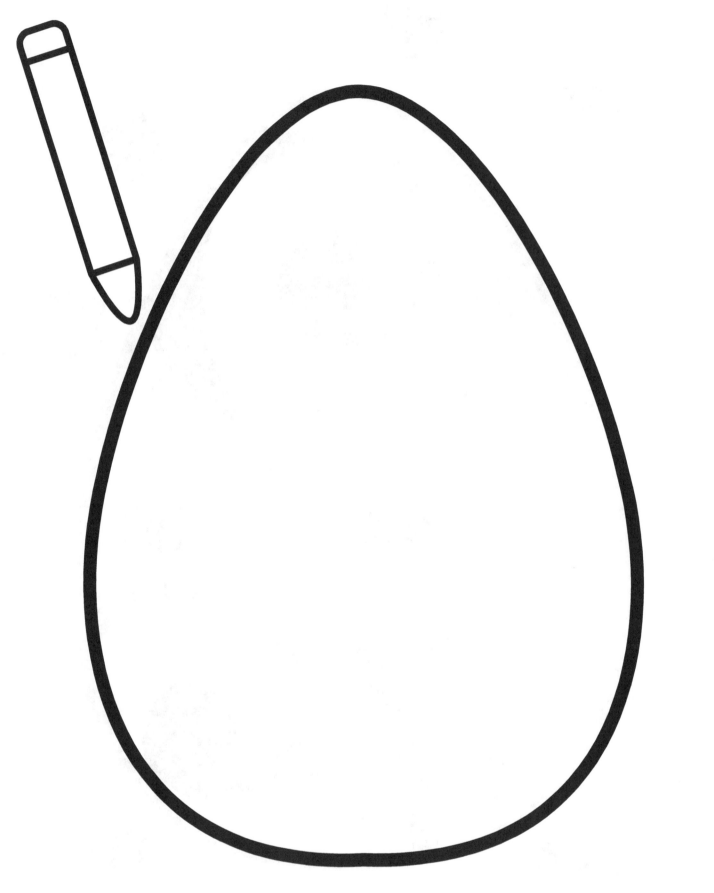

DRAW AND COLOR

HEY KIDS! DID YOU SEE OUR OTHER SUPER FUN EASTER COLORING BOOK?

My First Toddler Easter Coloring and Activity Book For kids Ages 2-8:

Starring Fun And Educational Numbers, Letters, Shapes, Scissor Skills And Animals

ASIN: 1777645808

SOME ARE EASY, AND SOME ARE CHALLENGING, BUT ALL RE FUN!!! HAVE AN ADULT SEARCH ON AMAZON USING HE ASIN NUMBER 1777645808.

R, SEARCH AMAZON USING "MAGICAL BEANS PRESS" O SEE ALL OUR COLOURING AND ACTIVITY BOOKS!

Made in United States
Troutdale, OR
04/15/2025

30588255R00031